POPULAR
ARTS
OF
COLONIAL
NEW MEXICO

by
E. Boyd
1959

MUSEUM
OF
INTERNATIONAL
FOLK ART
SANTA FE
NEW MEXICO

Cover Illustration—
Wool embroidery in *colcha* stitch
on woolen homespun.

Copyright 1959
Museum of International Folk Art
Santa Fe, New Mexico
Library of Congress Catalogue
Card No. 59-11399

The following pages briefly list arts and crafts of colonial New Mexico and how and why they were made. Sincere acknowledgment is tendered to the Board of the International Folk Art Foundation for its initiative and constructive action in making this publication possible.

E. BOYD.
Spanish Colonial Department,
Museum of New Mexico.
Santa Fe, New Mexico, 1959.

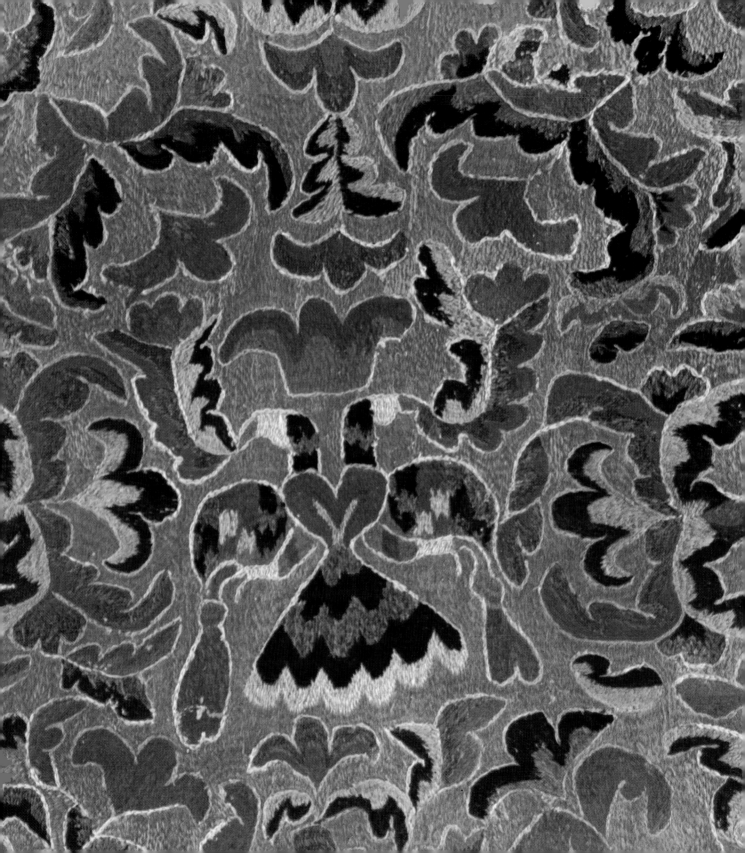

17TH CENTURY NEW MEXICO

Textbooks describe the explorations of Coronado in 1540 and settlement by Governor Oñate in 1598; New Mexico's next notice is its annexation by the United States in 1846. History names generals and governors, but during the apparently blank interval of 250 years, it was the courage, endurance, and resourcefulness of simple people that kept the colony alive and growing. Hostile Indians and extremes of climate in a giant-sized landscape that produced rude plenty made life perilous but worth fighting for. Centuries of battle with Islamic Arab invaders of the Iberian Peninsula and comparable climate and geography in Spain and New Mexico had equipped the Spaniards to adjust themselves to the conditions they found in the Rio Grande Valley.

From Arabia to Spain, building with sun-dried mud had been practiced for thousands of years as had the artificial diversion of streams to irrigate crops. In New Mexico the Pueblo Indians were already familiar with these techniques so that the Spanish had only to add a few improvements in architectural detail and employ Indian labor on their projects. Ten years after the establishment of a capital, which did not prove to be well located, it was removed to Santa Fe which is still the capital of New Mexico. The Casas Reales or seat of government, started in about 1610 after many vicissitudes, is today known as the Palace of the Governors, an adobe building one block long which has been for fifty years the home of the Museum of New Mexico.

Other than the massive walls of the Palace and early missions, no material objects from the 17th century exist except in the form of broken fragments excavated from ruins. The Pueblo Indians rebelled in 1680 and the Spanish who escaped death by surprise attack retreated in a body to El Paso, now Ciudad Juarez, Mexico.

Permanent reconquest took twelve years. When Governor General Diego de Vargas led the survivors of 1680 back to Santa Fe with his little army and the Franciscans delegated to return the peaceable Indians to "their two Majesties, the King of Heaven and the King of Spain," Indian submission was passively slow. The Casas Reales were rebuilt with an eye to defense first; architectural splendor could come later. Everything was to be built again. It was not until several years later that churches were replaced. In the interim, the Palace chapel served the Spanish population of Santa Fe as well as the military.

The oldest church is a title that has many claimants. The Santa Fe parish church had been torn down by the Indians who used its bricks to build a wall around the Palace and its water supply against the return of the Spanish, and to partition its rooms into their preferred little cubicles. It was not rebuilt until 1714. The great pre-1680 churches of Abo, Quarai, and Jemez whose walls loom up today were never rebuilt. Missions at Acoma and Isleta pueblos are said to have stood after their roofs were burned so that only new roofs were needed to put them in usable condition again. San Miguel Chapel at Santa Fe was built again from the ground up in 1710. One existing mission church, San José de la Laguna at Laguna Pueblo, may claim to have been built in the 17th century. Before 1680 Laguna did not exist; it is the one New Mexico pueblo that was founded after the Spanish came. Groups from Zuni, Cochiti, Cieneguilla, and possibly other pueblos, settled where there were good fields, a river, and a lake. The church was certainly begun in 1698-99 and completed by 1706. Not large nor pretentious, it has today the most beautiful and interesting interior of any in New Mexico and the people of Laguna are justly proud of having kept it so.

THE COLONIAL HOME OF THE 18TH CENTURY

The colonial home was of adobe. For warmth, security, and other reasons many members of the family slept in one room which, more often than not, was also the kitchen. Since every room had a corner fireplace, the kitchen was moved from a south- to a north-side room in summer. In spite of various claims to antiquity there are very few adobe structures in New Mexico today that are 150 years old or older. Weathering and roofing problems made it easier to build new rooms and let old ones go through a cycle of usage as storeroom, chicken house, or pigpen and rubbish dump. On the other hand, until sawmills and their products arrived in the 1870s, there was little change in house plans. Rooms were built in a row or an ell, or all around an inner patio. The *zaguan*, otherwise known as a dogtrot or breezeway, did not exist until southeasterners had moved to New Mexico after the Civil War. Rooms often opened on the outside but not from one room to another, a result of the unplanned additions to a parental home when new rooms were wanted for an extended family of married children.

The floor was always of packed earth, except in a very few churches where the sanctuary was floored with hand-hewn planks, wide and short and fitted together in blocks. Later on, a few enterprising people made similar wood floors such as may still be seen in the church of San José de Gracia at Trampas, New Mexico. In general, however, the floor was simply of dirt, and it was sprinkled each time that it was swept.

The fireplace was always in the corner of a room and its hearth was more or less a quarter-circle arc. The early missions had large, hooded "stoves" made with a stone stove top, built-in ovens and poles and mud plaster. These were makeshift versions of the carved stone and tiled brick cookstoves of medieval Mediterranean countries. Some Spanish colonials continued to build the pole and mud hood in their homes into the 19th century but discarded the stove in favor of an open corner hearth which gave more heat. Pueblo Indians also adopted the hood, leveling its pitched slope so that foods could be dried on the flat top which also made a warm bed for sleeping. Corner fireplaces were small, giving the maximum heat for the fuel consumed. No fireplace was set flush in the middle of a wall as is the northern European custom, but sometimes one was built on a long wall with a low crosswall on the open side forming a draft-stop and making in effect a corner fireplace with a quarter-arc hearth.

Doors were small, averaging five feet in height, with sills raised above ground and lintels below normal stature so that to pass through one had to step high and bend low. This is said to have been a protection against Indian attack, but was as much to keep flood waters out and warmth inside. To avoid wasteful use of iron for hinges, doors were of puncheon style that swung, or dragged, on the sill. The typical colonial door of the 18th century has survived in New Mexico in only one place: the Santuario of Chimayo. Characteristically, this chapel was built in 1816 but in the style of the previous century. Doors of the same design made earlier and exposed to weathering were long ago replaced by newer models in New Mexico. However, doors of the same design but carved of hard wood and on a grander scale still exist in Mexican churches. One of the same pattern was found in restoration of Mission San José, near San Antonio, Texas, which dates from about 1740. Faithful reproductions of it have been installed in other restored missions at San Antonio and in its Palace of the Governors. This type of door is composed of square and rectangular panels set in cross directions, giving an effect of the Greek key motif. The panels are carved in relief with crests as are the framing moldings. At the Santuario in Chimayo, the doors are between the chapel and narthex, and so were protected from the weather.

The small paneled door is the one which lasted into our time, with a thick panel or pairs of them beveled at the edges to fit into the slotted frame, and as a rule, no decoration. A door made of a solid slab of hand-adzed wood with a band of simple chiseled elements across the center was also used but its structure was apt to warp and check. Shutters and storage alcoves had smaller doors of the same patterns, all of the puncheon type.

Windows were small, set high in the wall and unglazed unless with panes of native selenite measuring about four by four inches, which were set between narrow stringers so that they overlapped. These let in light but were not transparent. Heavy outer shutters were for security and kept out cold.

18th century type of
pine chest on stand.
(Page 9)

Lighting was chiefly that of the sun or fire. In paintings on tanned buffalo skins of about 1700, we see various types of lighting devices: hanging metal oil lamps, a tall candlestick, pierced metal lanterns, and flaming torches. As these regional paintings are thought to have been painted by Franciscan priests newly come from Mexico or Spain (see p. 21), the lamps and torches may well have been typical of their time, but as yet, there is no evidence that such objects were ever seen in New Mexico. What they had were candlesticks, of wood, pewter, copper, brass, silver, or iron. The fact that a church might own four or ten at most would suggest that these were scarce. The *araña*, or spider, was a hanging chandelier either circular or merely of two wooden crosspieces with holes for candles bored in them. A more elegant, if small, form of chandelier is of iron with candlesockets on arms and a wrought iron bird at the top. One of these was used in the Palace of the Governors in Spanish times and is still to be seen there.

Furniture and Furnishings

Furniture was country-made for most of the people. Legends of the grand style kept by the governors may have been true in some cases, but it is obvious that their carved chairs, tapestry hangings, and silver came with them from Mexico and returned there when they left. After De Vargas very few governors died in office.

Beds did not exist for country folk. They slept on woolsacks and sheep pelts, each person wrapped in a blanket. By day the blankets hung over a pole suspended from the ceiling while woolsacks were propped against the walls for daytime lounging. This custom was still in vogue in Santa Fe in 1846 when Susan Magoffin described it.(1) *

Chairs were for prestige, reserved for officials and priests. In the parish church of Santa Fe in 1776 Father Dominguez made an inventory (2) and wrote: "On the wall opposite . . . is the lord governor's seat. This is an armchair (it belongs to the government but I mention what is there) of fine wood upholstered in crimson velvet with galloon and fringe of fine gold, all affixed by nails of gilt metal. The cushion matches the chair, with tassels at the corners."

In Mexico a bishop's throne was large and ornate, but in New Mexico

---

*Numbers in parentheses refer to the reference list on page 51.

the priest's chair was of sturdy pine with a simply railed or splatted back and apron and open, angled arms, usually chiseled in traditional geometric bands, mortised and tenoned without nails. If not very comfortable, these chairs are still handsome in a rustic way. These were kept behind the sanctuary rail in church, and in homes perhaps one was kept for visits of the priest.

The absence of chairs was by no means a New Mexican peculiarity. Their use by others than royalty and clerics began only at the end of the 17th century in Europe. An inventory of the contents of a Mexico City house in 1780, whose owners were prominent and wealthy, listed many sofas, about ninety upholstered and wooden stools and only two or three chairs, one of which was reserved solely as an easel to display the portrait of the reigning king of Spain. (3)

A table is unhandy for persons sitting on the floor, so serving tables in New Mexico were low, little, and rather like a footstool or modern coffee table. A solid pine top was mortised to the stumpy legs and braced with a scrolled and grooved apron. The churches took to using rough lumber altars of wood to be covered with linens in place of earlier adobe altars, and another large deal table, sometimes with a box or two built under it, served in the sacristy for vesting.

The *tarima* or stool was versatile and expendable. The word was used for the adobe ledge built indoors or outside against a wall as a seat, as well as for a plain slab of pine with four pole legs set in it. Correctly, the small footstool is a *tarimita* which was made of five pieces; two ends mortised to the top acted as legs and a pair of aprons served as braces; as a rule there was no decoration. These were movable and used at home, in church, and in wagons.

The *trastero* or great cupboard was the principal piece of furniture. Often more than seven feet high, it had a carved shell crest and two pairs of doors, one with open grille of hand-carved spindles and the other of solid panels. Within were shelves and shoebox-shaped drawers. Sometimes half of these were "secret," as in the secretaries of the Old World, so that one had to remove an inner box to get at the hidden drawers. As colonial life tended to a democratic level of active labor and lack of wealth, the *trastero* grew smaller, discarded drawers, and was used to store food and dishes. At the end of the 18th century it was made without so much carved detail, but retained the carved shell crest and was covered with gesso and painted with the same motifs that were used in religious decorations.

Chests were of many sizes and served for storage, traveling boxes, and other purposes. In the 18th century they were carved in low relief with lions, rosettes, pomegranates, and scrolls of an earlier century on massive pine slabs, each of which served as a side, lid, or bottom. These stood on removable wooden stands. Large boxes for church vestments often had small "drawers," actually separate boxes, in them to hold little things. Other chests with paneled fronts had built-in legs and were not intended to be carried about.

In iron-poor New Mexico there was never the abundance of fancy ironwork which we associate with Spain and its colonies. Blacksmiths could not indulge in making wastefully ornamental pieces but had to keep plough points, axes, the adz, hoe, sword, and lance in serviceable condition. The most-used hinge for boxes and cupboards was a pair of interlocked eyes of iron whose pointed ends spread out as they were driven into wood. Hasps and scutcheons, if used at all, were small, plain, and crudely ornamented with stamped dots and semicircles.

The grain chest was immense with built-in legs, heavy plain panels, and often multiple compartments, although villagers sometimes hollowed out a cottonwood log and caulked the ends to serve the same purpose.

Traveling boxes if not of pine were of rawhide, heavily ironbound and decorated with patches of bright velvet or baize laced on with buckskin thongs.

Trinket boxes sometimes came from Michoacan, Mexico, and were of lacquer or of carved wood. In New Mexico, candles and trinkets were kept in little boxes of rawhide, or of pine decorated with cut straw and corn husks.

Ornamental straw work is a craft with an ancient history since it was practiced by peasants of North Africa for centuries before the Moors brought it to Spain. Like many other Moorish or Arab arts, it was adopted by Spanish artisans who carried it to the New World and to the upper

Rio Grande Valley. Straw decoration was the poor man's gilding on boxes, panels, wooden candleholders, picture moldings, hanging shelves, and devotional wooden crosses. New Mexicans made use of the gleaming natural golden color of dried wheat straw and corn husks and cut these into fine bits which were affixed by means of the rosin-soot mixture that also served to color the wood surface black. Unlike Europeans of the 18th century, they never dyed straw in colors. "Straw inlay" is a misnomer which has persisted, but inlay was not done; the straw was simply pasted on in designs of flowers and geometric shapes, often including the cross.

Hanging shelves were in every room to hold the family saints' images, candles, and paper flowers. Of natural wood or gessoed and painted with tempera, they had one or two shelves and a scrolled or cut-out apron. A few might have had wooden pegs or wrought-iron hooks on which to hang hats, shawls, lariats, and strings of dried vegetables below the shelf.

Cooking was done in three places: in outdoor barbecue pits, in outdoor beehive-shaped adobe ovens, and in the fireplace. Because there was no space for a crane or roasting spit or dripping pan, the pot that was to boil stood over a plain iron trivet or *tinamaiste* while things to be kept warm stood on raked-out coals or merely on the warm adobe hearth.

Baking of *tortillas*, the indispensable patted cakes of wheat flour or corn meal, was done on a hot stone slab or iron or copper griddle. The perennial value set on homely metal utensils is underlined in a will made in 1762 by Juana Romero, a widow of Cieneguilla. (4) Presumably on her deathbed, she left instructions for the care of her children, then named those to receive her belongings: "My two cows and a calf, my loom with its shuttles and wool cards, my *iron griddle and two iron spoons.*" Such iron spoons were of the European, round-bowl form with simple rattail handle or a peculiar, two-bowl spoon, one of which is turned up and one down no matter which way it is held. For the most part spoons, ladles, scoops, and dippers were made of wood, horn, and gourd rinds; the *tortilla*, like medieval trencher bread, often served as plate and spoon before it was eaten.

Cooking vessels were chiefly of Pueblo Indian manufacture. If they were not high-fired and durable, there were always more to be had. The majolica and Chinese porcelain cups and plates which trickled into New

Bulto, a bishop, tempera
paint over gesso coated
cottonwood root.
(Page 31)

Mexico effected changes in shape and design of Indian pottery, or at least that made for the Spanish; dishes had soup plate rims, and flaring cups were made with footed base. Ornamental painting adopted roses, lilies, crosses, concentric circles, and other details not found in prehistoric Indian pottery.

Coppers from Mexico came in all sizes of open kettle from the tiny to the caldron. The smaller coppers were carried by Cortez's army in 1520 and by riders for centuries after, serving as washbasin and cook pot. Gypsies had a monopoly on copperwork and its repair in Spain, and it is probable that gypsies who came to Mexico set up in their traditional craft there. The town of Santa Clara de Cobre in Mexico still turns out hand-made copper articles in traditional shapes although the techniques are not quite the same.

The traditional drinking mug from Peru to New Mexico was the copper *chocolatero* with free rattail handle. Plates, bowls, and pitchers of handsome shape were also brought from Mexico. The life of a worn-out copper kettle was prolonged on the frontier by riveting copper scrap over holes until the entire bottom was scaled like a shingle roof.

Utensils that did not come in contact with fire, such as jugs, bowls, and bottles, were devised from nonedible gourds raised for the purpose. Other bowls, dough troughs, cheese presses, and the like were fashioned of wood.

Textiles

Spinning and weaving required wheels and looms. Country-made, these were large and clumsy. Although sometimes set up outside, most of them were used indoors, for the cold winters were the time when there was less work in the fields. The spinning wheel was an oversized sawhorse of rough log on three legs on which were a wooden wheel and pair of prongs to hold a bobbin. If wheels of this kind had been used by the Pilgrims who landed at Plymouth Rock in 1620, there would not today be so many spinning wheels in the United States which "came over on the Mayflower."

Looms in New Mexico seem to have been made to weave wool yarns. While cotton was raised and spun by prehistoric Southwesterners, and painted cotton blankets were worn by Pueblo Indians when Coronado first saw them, it is still a matter of doubtful certainty whether the Spanish ever wove any cotton. Pueblo Indians continued to weave *mantas* of cotton for annual tribute and for themselves, as the Hopi still do for ceremonial garments, but in the meantime they had learned sheep management and the uses of wool. At Isleta Pueblo in 1776 a little cotton was raised, it was said, to make candlewicks. (2)

The Spanish brought with them Merino sheep, a leggy breed whose yield per clip was small, but the springy twist in each wool fiber spun up into fine, silky yarn which gave great warmth for its light weight. Colonial spinning along the northern Rio Grande was not as fine as that done in some parts of Mexico. New Mexicans used wool warps and wefts while many of the most intricately patterned Mexican textiles employed warps of the native varieties of maguey or agave. These permitted more threads to the inch and more fancy-patterned weaving.

Textiles of 18th-century New Mexico have not survived the ravages of moths, mice, and men, but archives frequently mention them, and in many ways they were probably the same as those of later years with the exception of those made after commercial dyes could be obtained. Weaving was practiced all over New Mexico by necessity until factory-made goods became available, when it died out except in a few of the more remote mountain areas to the north. The best-known weaving center continued to make novelty textiles on modern looms and still does so; it is the region around Chimayo. As a result, for nearly fifty years all of the older blankets were called Chimayo blankets, but recently the more correct term, Rio Grande blankets, has come into use. The Rio Grande blanket was made of two narrow lengths either sewn together down the middle or woven together by carrying threads over the warps, which produced a ridge down the center. The selvedges have multiple warps and are not finished with the looped yarn trim used on Indian-made blankets.

Presence of the lazy stitch, where a weaver has worked up the warps in one part of the work without weaving at the same level all the way across, is a sure indication that the textile is Indian and not Spanish. The harness loom does not admit of this way of weaving, while it is convenient on the vertical loom used by Navajo and Hopi. These clues are often the only way to distinguish between Spanish and Indian blankets made when the same dyes and nearly the same ticked and striped patterns were used by both.

Blankets were used at night, wrapped around each person, and by day served as overcoats. They were carried folded over the shoulder when not in use, like a Scotch tartan, and worn over the head and around the shoulders as Taos Indians do today, instead of having a slit at the center to drop the blanket on the shoulders as do Mexican *sarapes* or *ponchos*. These blankets were soft and light and were not intended to be used as rugs. For this purpose a coarser yarn was spun and woven into the *jerga*. The *jerga* (also spelled *gerga* or *xerga*) was woven in lengths about two feet wide and sewn together so that the floor was covered wall to wall with this carpet, usually a diagonal twill but sometimes herringbone or diamond weave. The common kind was of light and dark natural wool colors, but some were dyed solid crimson with cochineal. Others were made in a variety of colors in stripes, checks, and plaids. It is obvious that different weavers sat at the loom while one length was in process as changes in direction of the twill and even of the pattern appear and then switch back to the original plan. Carpets in church sanctuaries were mentioned by Dominguez (2) and in 1787 at Santa Cruz (5) where one was noted as "one *gerga*, new, of colors." Some sort of coarse saddle blanket of which no specimen is recorded today was also called *jerga*.

Sabanilla or plain-weave homespun in natural finespun yarn was made for many purposes. Dyed with indigo, it made men's breeches, women's skirts, and Franciscan habits. Sewn into a sack and stuffed with raw wool it made a matress. It was the fabric on which the solid, allover wool embroidery of the *colcha* was done.

Using the same range of vegetable dyes as the Rio Grande blankets, the *colcha* was a richly colorful hanging, worked in various geometric patterns, wavy bands alternating with flowers, or large scrolled leaves and flowers all over the design. These country-made substitutes for tapestries are recorded as having been in the Chapel of Our Lady of Light, or Castrense, in .Santa Fe in 1776 (2), and they may have looked like a surviving example which has the double-headed eagle at its center. Although too perishable for the purpose, they were also used as carpets in chapels for lack of more suitable ones. In Spanish, *colcha* means a quilt, but these

Trastero, pine cupboard painted
in tempera over gesso.
(Page 12)

embroideries on wool obviously were not quilts. On the other hand, the stitch employed on them is somewhat of a mystery in that its counterpart is not found in earlier or contemporary folk embroideries of Spain and Mexico. It is a series of parallel long stitches tacked down with a short, diagonal point. If the designs were taken from embroideries in silks which were to be seen on Mexican and Chinese altar cloths of the period, their transference into wool yarns may have inspired the cross-tack stitch to hold the yarn in place, which gave a quilted effect. In any case, the *colcha* stitch seems to have been strictly a New Mexican improvisation. (6)

Costume

Costume of the 18th-century colonial epoch in New Mexico no longer exists, but limited materials and improvised tailoring produced garments of far simpler styles than those worn in Mexico, where fashion-model dolls arrived from Madrid, London, or Paris. Men wore blue wool breeches over a cotton shirt and drawers; some might have had a long blue coat over a vest of red Manchester cloth or buckskin, with a stocking cap or flat-crowned, medium-brimmed leather hat. Knitted stockings, moccasins like the Indian's except that they closed in front, and *botas* completed the man's dress. Boots were not worn; for riding, the legs were protected by the *botas*, soft leather flaps which were tied on at the knee and covered the leg and foot. In Mexico these were elegantly made of tooled leather embroidered with metal thread and braid, but New Mexicans made them of buckskin with red baize facings. A man carried his knife and cigarette makings in his sash. The sword hung from its own belt. Bullets, powder horn made of a cow's horn, and flints were carried in an embroidered leather pouch slung by a strap over the shoulder.

Women wore a cotton chemise doubling as blouse under full woolen skirts and wrapped up in a shawl or *reboso*, in the folds of which they carried babies, bundles, and cigarette makings.

RELIGIOUS ART OF THE 18TH CENTURY

Soon after the reconquest in 1692, perhaps while temporary chapels were in use, a few Franciscans with talent and resourcefulness began to paint pictures on tanned buffalo hides as a supplement to their missionary labors. The hides were plentiful in New Mexico and so were their other materials: indigo and native vegetal dyes used by the Indians to color buckskin. The pictures were of the Crucifix and of Mary, Joseph, St. John the Baptist, and the principal Franciscan saints. If the materials were crude, the Franciscans' skill in drawing was well developed. They drew in the Renaissance style which was well out of fashion in Europe, but large murals painted in true fresco had been lavished on various convents and churches of Mexico in the 16th century, and these the friars may well have known before they came to New Mexico.

Like handwriting, personal mannerisms in drawing and painting are identifiable from one picture to another even if the artist is unknown. The earlier paintings on hides are the best drawn and limited in subject matter. Throughout the 18th century other such paintings were made by less able artists. These either copied the earlier subjects imperfectly or painted saints, or miracle statues, of more regional popularity or more recent canonization.

Hundreds of religious paintings on hides are noted in 18th-century inventories of churches and in wills of private individuals in New Mexico. Ecclesiastical visitors from Mexico made caustic comments on the unseemliness of animal hides as backgrounds for holy images. In time the now dusty skins were cut up into sacks, used for bookbinding of church records or simply for patching. Secular clerics, after republican Mexico was established, ordered the removal of what was left of the offending material in 1826. (5) Today, just over forty paintings of this class are known, some of which are only fragmentary. Some of these have appeared from neglected storerooms and secret hiding places in the past twelve years. It is hoped that there are still others waiting to be discovered. After more than a century of abuse, the powerful style and ingenious qualities of this unique form of colonial art are appreciated and sought after.

Retablo, The Holy Child of
Atocha, painted in tempera on
gesso coated pine panel.
(Page 31)

Academic or Priestly Sculpture and Painting

The King's fund and pious individuals provided images from Mexico, but as more churches were built and more people filled them there was a need for more images. Not all the Franciscans felt happy in New Mexico during their tours of duty there, but some certainly were filled with zeal and a love for their congregations. Of these Fray Andres Garcia, who came to the upper Rio Grande in 1747, was one. (2) During his thirty-two years of service he was at fourteen pueblos and at Abiquiu, Santa Cruz, and Albuquerque. Where he stayed for any time, he made pictures and statues for the mission, carving and painting them himself. He also made altar railings, pulpits, canopies, and tabernacles where they were lacking. If he was not a genius, he had good will and a few of his figures are still in the church for which he made them, for instance, the "Christ in the Sepulcher" at the Santa Cruz church.

Fray Juan Jose Toledo, in New Mexico between 1743 and 1772, also made statues in the round described by Dominguez: ".... and it is ugly enough, but very much adorned with little ribbon flowers and ordinary small medals." (2) Paintings in oil on gessoed wood panels in rather delicate, rosy style are not all alike, so more than one friar was at work at the time. However, their iconography is conventional and the painting follows the minor baroque style of Mexico. Three of these panels bear names of their donors and the inscribed dates of 1754, 1780, and 1783.

An oil painting of St. Michael on canvas in a rough, boldly brushed, if amateurishly drawn, composition is owned by the Chapel of San Miguel, Santa Fe. In general, it is copied from one of the theatrical paintings of the same subject by professional Mexican painters of the period. The date is not given on it, but the name and title of its donor provide a clue: Don Miguel Saenz de Garvisu, commander of the garrison at the Royal Presidio of Santa Fe. He held this post from 1745 to 1749. The vigorous style of the anonymous artist reminds us that there was at least one layman in Santa Fe who practiced art in several forms.

Panels of relief built up with gesso were another form of 18th-century colonial folk art. Most of the examples in existence appear to be by one person although a few are more naive in composition. Gesso relief incorporated into painted panels was traditional in Gothic art, and continued in conservative Spain into the 16th century. A very different use of free-standing gesso relief was that of the flamboyant rococo period of the 18th century. Which of these phases inspired the New Mexican panels is uncertain, for their overall expression is folk-rococo. To carve relief from a rosinous pine slab is difficult; the building up of thick gesso achieved a better result. Heads of the images were carved in wood in half round and gessoed into place, while other raised areas were modeled with the plaster. The composition and iconography of these are traditional, and the colors of most of them, if not overpainted in modern oils, are pleasing.

Franciscan churches of New Mexico had painted walls behind the altar. Excavations in the ruins of missions at Awatovi and at Jemez exposed painted designs in water-soluble paints on the mud plaster. These resembled glazed tile and wrought iron, or patterns from European textiles. Traces of the same style of painting have been found on the sanctuary wall at Laguna mission and in San Miguel Chapel, Santa Fe. At Domingo Pueblo in 1776, Fr. Dominguez described the high altar there: "Father Zamora had a small altar screen in perspective painted on the wall at his own expense. Although it is an ordinary tempera painting, it is very pretty and carefully done. It is in two sections and does not reach the ceiling. . . . Painted on either side of the screen as though in niches are . . . St. Francis and St. John Nepomuk." (2) This style was also practiced in Sonora, California, and Texas but the painting was often done on hard plaster and so more of it has survived in spite of neglect. But a great change in altar adornment was to take place after 1760, when the carved stone altar screen of the Chapel of Our Lady of Light was built in Santa Fe at that time. Governor Francisco Marin del Valle and his wife felt that their devotion to their faith might best be expressed by building a new church in more seemly architectural style than those they found in Santa Fe. The Chapel of Our Lady of Light was intended for the use of the military which at that time included the Governor, his entourage of the Palace, and the more prominent citizens, nearly all of whom held some military rank in the local militia. Although built of adobe like the rest of Santa Fe, this chapel had stone steps and paving in its sanctuary, a stone

The typical costume of a New Mexican colonial man is worn by this image of *Santiago*, or St. James the Apostle, the patron of Spain. (Collection of Mrs. C. G. Thompson).

(Page 20)

pulpit, carved stone reliefs on the facade and altar frontal, and a great carved stone altar screen. In order to have such work done, Governor Marin de Valle brought stone masons from Mexico, possibly from Zacatecas since that was his home town, and it is said that when the chapel was finished the masons returned to Mexico for there was no more employment for them in Santa Fe.

If the stone altarpiece of the Castrense or military chapel does not measure up to the sophisticated and lavish carving and architectural design of many Mexican buildings, it is certainly the most imposing and ambitious piece of work to be done in colonial New Mexico. Today it stands in the new adobe Church of Cristo Rey at Santa Fe, a building planned around the stone reredos, and with the polychromed painting softened by time, it is perhaps more handsome and impressive than when it was new. The plan is one seen in church architecture from Mexico to Chile and was used as much for the facade as for an altar screen. Pilasters support bands of relief carving and pediments, and frame panels which here contain images of the saints in relief, but in other examples, framed statues in the round and paintings on canvas. Basically this is a Renaissance style of architectural ornament, but it has an overlay of the Churriguerresque which at its most elaborate covered every inch of surface with decoration. Provincial limitations gave to the Castrense altarpiece a certain restraint which to modern taste is more desirable.

New Mexican religious folk art began to bloom as the new ideas presented by the stone altarpiece took root in the minds of native-born colonial craftsmen. Such splendor in the Castrense made other churches look shabby and bare. If stone was a material that they could not or would not work, the elements of the screen could be translated into wood: pediments, cornices, pilasters, and panels. By 1776 the Santa Fe parish church, Santa Cruz and Zuni, Taos and San Juan pueblos had altar screens of wood. These Fr. Dominguez described as poor or hideous except at Santa Fe where he was more tolerant of the effect. (2) None of these screens at that time had images painted directly on them; they were simply to set off the statues and pictures already owned by each church.

Such a wooden reredos is to be seen in San Miguel Chapel, Santa Fe, presented by Don Antonio José Ortiz in 1798, which fact was recorded in two cartouches painted in the same location as the carved stone plaques on the Castrense altarscreen bearing the names of Governor Marin del Valle and his wife and the date of their benefaction. The San Miguel screen, of hand-hewn timbers stoutly mortised and doweled together, was carefully designed to display six paintings on canvas, a finely carved *estofado* statue of St. Michael, the patron saint, which had come from Mexico by 1709, and two smaller statues now lost. The gilded St. Michael stood in the central niche; the smaller figures on brackets, and the paintings of varied sizes were framed with painted floral scrolls in freely brushed shades of rose and soft green. No painting could be moved to another place on the screen since the wood behind each one was thriftily left unpainted.

After thirty-five years the flat pilasters of the Castrense screen were replaced on the San Miguel altarpiece by Salomonic columns, a style that continued to be popular in New Mexican *santero* altarscreens for some time. Except for the carved wooden shells at the top and small painted grapevines on the columns, there is no religious symbolism on the reredos at San Miguel; the painted surface bears the same floral motifs which folk artists had been using to decorate cupboards and chests.

Santos and Santeros

By 1800, image makers were busily providing saints in the round and painted on little panels and great altarscreens. Once these could be obtained at home instead of from some workshop twelve or fifteen hundred miles away, everyone wanted his own saints and saints for his own church. The colonials, already accustomed to work with wood and gesso and to making their own colors, had only to extend their skills to depict the holy images. In this respect their liturgical knowledge, when uncertain or inadequate, was often supplemented by delightfully improvised departures from the European Christian symbols in art. Carved figures in a few years assumed poses of hieratic dignity quite different from the animated and exaggerated action of Mexican models to be seen in the churches. Painting was adjusted to its local materials; the opaque, dark backgrounds were abandoned, and the white gesso ground was left untouched where white or light areas were wanted. Overpainting and corrective retouching were

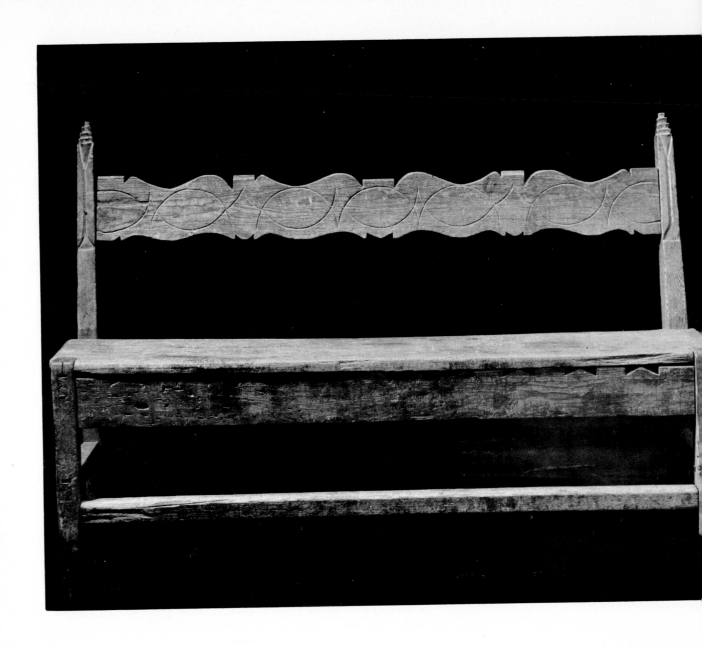

Pine bench of colonial design.
(Page 44)

practically never done by native *santeros*. To work in this method using transparent color on white background requires skill and forethought which come only with experience. If the *santero* concentration of interest in the meaning of the image led him to discard perspective, anatomy, and the third dimension, it seems to have been deliberate and not merely due to incompetence. Unlike the Franciscans a century before, the indigenous New Mexican folk artists supplied symbols of saintly virtues, of the Sacraments, and of basic truths in the religion of their patrons. For them a mere symbol was enough, while the missionaries had depicted episodes of the New Testament and the principal characters to serve as graphic extensions of their preachments to converts still being instructed in a new religion.

The word *santo* has in the past few decades been appropriated rather rashly by New Mexicans to indicate the images made by Spanish folk artists, but in universal Spanish the word has broader definitions. As an adjective, *santo* means holy. As a noun it may mean a holy person or saint, or an image of one. This image may be made in any material: stone, wood, plaster, metal, paper, and so on. The image in the round is *un santo de bulto*, or *de talla*, while a painted, printed, or flat image is *un santo de retablo*.

The maker of images is *un santero* and his workshop is *una santería*. In colonial archives the word *santo* was used as an adjective while the word *imagen*, or *ymagen*, was applied to the images. Nineteenth-century English-speaking diarists in New Mexico spoke disparagingly of the folk art they found, describing the figures as wax dolls, an extraordinarily defective observation since wax images were not made in New Mexico, but most of the "Anglos" had seen wax-headed dolls in the eastern states, and so jumped to conclusions. The use of the word *santo* in English does not appear in print until well after 1900 when artists and collectors began to admire their fine color and primitive form.

Materials and implements for making images were no different from those already in use for other purposes: the small Spanish ax, adz, knife, oversized awl, a serrated knife blade, a chisel or two, chunks of fine and coarse sandstone which were used in place of sandpaper for smoothing, quill pens, sometimes a compass, brushes made of hog bristles, pine, well-seasoned roots of cottonwood, gesso made of native gypsum and glue, and colors. Indigo, cochineal, and occasionally vermilion were imported, but other reds were made from native iron oxide. Yellows were sometimes mineral from ocher, but more often of vegetable origin. (7) From these, green and purple could be mixed and the dark areas were a mixture of all of them; for example, indigo mixed with dark brown is the actual color found in nearly all *santero* painting instead of black, except in backgrounds for decorative straw work. True black seems hardly ever to have been made, although ingredients such as bone, charcoal, and soot were certainly available. Micaceous earth called *tierra amarilla*, which had been used to give glitter to Indian pottery and to wall plaster in colonial homes, was sometimes mixed with parts of the colors to give a golden glint to areas like a robe or framing element.

In spite of the common use of the term "egg tempera" in connection with New Mexico folk arts, analysis has not confirmed the use of egg in the pigment mixture. The colors seem to have been water colors in a true sense and accordingly vulnerable to water damage. Early enthusiasts wrote of the beautiful "golden glow" painted on some *retablos;* in fact, this was not a part of the painting at all, but the mellowed rosin varnish used by the *santero* himself. With time this pure film, distilled from native pitch pine, turns golden and has a fine crackle, but it had the great virtue of not turning dark, gummy brown like commercial varnishes. These, in coarse forms, have been applied to many *santos* but were not used by the original makers.

The *santero* worked his farm, ran his mill, or tended his animals as did his neighbors and made images in his spare time or in winter when there was little to do out of doors. Contrary to legend he did not make a cartload, nor a burroload, of images and then peddle them over the countryside. Instead, he would receive one or more commissions from a village, and if it were any distance from home, he would pack up his work kit and his family and go there to stay until his orders were filled. While he was on the spot he usually received more orders, for everyone wanted an image of his particular devotion.

The census was never very reliable in New Mexico, but between 1800 and 1846 the Spanish, the half-caste, and the Christian Indian population was estimated to have been from 26,000 upward to 43,000 in round figures. It is conservative to state that there must at one time have been as many *santos*, not counting the great altarpieces and the many others of Mexican origin. Not only did everyone own one, but each house kept several in each room. While the Pueblo Indians did not make *santos* themselves except in rare instances, they had just as many in their missions and homes as the Spanish. In fact they kept them in decent, respected state for many decades longer than did their Spanish neighbors.

San José mission at Laguna Pueblo received a new painted wooden altarpiece sometime between 1800 and 1809. While the larger altarscreen in Acoma Pueblo's church was done at approximately the same time, it has been recently and amateurishly overpainted. However, the construction of the two and the layout of panels are clearly by the same artist and, equally clearly, adapted from the stone screen of the Castrense. Two painted ovals on the lower pediment must originally have contained the donor's name and date of making, just as was lettered on the stone prototype. Unfortunately at Laguna these were long ago scrubbed away in annual cleaning and have been lately filled in with the Franciscan emblem.

The style of brushwork, the co-ordination of the limited color range into a composition that glows with rich warmth, and the boldly planned use of architectural detail in the round and in paint make the Laguna piece the finest and most beautiful *santero* period piece that exists today. Obviously the folk artist had done previous work to justify his commission for these two churches and to enable him to execute them so successfully. Although anonymous, his hand is identifiable in a group of rather large single panels, usually depicting half-length figures. It is quite possible that these substantially painted single specimens won the painter the commissions for Acoma and Laguna.

The *bulto* or statue in the round is hard to date or identify by its style. *Bultos* were not signed and all too many have been repaired and overpainted. One example, of course, exists to disprove the rule: an ambitious architectural pedestal for a figure of the Virgin of Refuge in the Taylor Museum bears the painted date 1820. (8)

After the Santuario at Chimayo was completed in 1816, a set of nine figures was made for it. Of those still in place, the Crucifix, the Nazarene

Christ, the Archangel Rafael, the now famous small Santiago on his white horse, and several advocations of the Virgin share lively, intelligent expressions, sharply carved planes, and clear, pure coloring. Light blue and grey eyes are another differentiation from many other physical types depicted in regional images. One of the figures of the Virgin of Sorrows with hollow-frame skirt and wide, despairing grey eyes, which was formerly in the Santa Cruz church, was of this type.

Both hard work and ingenuity were required in the making of a *bulto*. Well-dried cottonwood root, as soft to carve as balsa, was shaped into the many sections required for head, torso, upper and forearms, sometimes separate hands, legs, or robe, and as required, feet, a pedestal, wings, and nimbus as well as various attributes. Pegged together and covered with smoothed-over gesso, these were ready to paint if not of more complicated nature. For figures which required drapery folds or a mantle over the head, cloth soaked in thick wet gesso was molded over the wood by hand and allowed to set before painting. If a wide court skirt was required, it was made of cloth and gesso stretched over a frame of small poles and sticks. The hollow-frame skirt not only saved extensive carving of a large block of pine but reduced weight when the image was carried in processions. The corpus of a Crucifix large enough to be taken from the cross and placed in its sepulcher on Holy Friday, when it was carried about the village, was made with leather joints. Neither the hollow frame nor the jointed figure was invented by New Mexicans; they were well known in professional workshops in Mexican towns where they were made by academically trained craftsmen.

Images dressed in fabric garments were traditional in Spain and her colonies. It is true that it was customary to lavish the most costly textiles, gold and silver lace, and gems on the images of the mother country, and insofar as it was possible New Mexicans did the same in the 18th century. The most venerated statues of the Virgin of the Rosary and of Carmel then owned silk and velvet gowns, hammered silver crowns and nimbus, coral and silver rosaries and even "a little silver dog and two silver toothpicks." (5) As colonial economy shifted from barter to cash and rural standards of living declined, the villagers continued to dress their favorite *santos* in whatever they could find: machine-stitched calico Mother Hub-

Chair and table of pine
with traditional New
Mexico proportions.
(Page 44)

bards, beads, crochet sacques, a doll's hat, tinsel, and any other offering at hand. Currently, country chapel images are seen decked in necklace and bracelets of plastic lacing or rayon socks. By the mid-19th century, effort was no longer expended on carving elaborate surface detail of figures; it was concentrated on heads and hands. Conical torsos were painted on the front and were often plain red or blue on the reverse.

It is safe to say that the most delicately carved, rather pretty, and iconographically conventional *bultos* that exist today are the oldest made by New Mexicans. As confidence and stylization produced simpler but more distinctive forms, iconography was lost sight of or confused. A strong trend toward carving faces which although nonnaturalistic are typical of Spanish New Mexican physical types today suggests that later *santeros* took their family and neighbors for guides if not actual models. The faint but visible influence of vanished Gothic, Renaissance, and baroque styles disappeared and a *bulto* acquired a human, rather than a heavenly, personality.

Specialized types of figures were made for the Brothers of Light, a society of penitents who claim to have continued as members of the Third Order of St. Francis of Assisi founded by him for laymen. Each meeting house, called a *morada*, that was maintained by a local chapter of penitents, required *bultos* to represent the chief characters of the Passion. Briefly limited to effigies of the Nazarene Christ, the Crucifix, the Sorrowing Virgin, and Christ in the Sepulcher, with Death in her cart as a rule, these were turned out in sets, and except for starkly emotional faces and gory detail, had little variety or delicacy of execution. Intended to wear cloth garments they were blocked out and often unfinished below the neck. Arms jointed by rags allowed easy change of garments. Oil paint and window glass for eyes were now accessible and used. The roster of saints and painted *retablos* was not required, but when New Mexico folk art began to be cleared out of churches to be replaced by commercially made images the *santos* found a refuge in many *moradas* no matter what saints they represented.

DECLINE IN THE 19TH CENTURY

Spain's ban on trade between her colonies and other countries began to weaken before Mexico declared her independence in 1821. The new republic soon made trade agreements with foreign nations including England. The nearest market place for New Mexico was Chihuahua City where a great annual fair had been licensed in 1806. In its early years, New Mexico sent bales of hides, woven blankets, and thousands of sheep on the hoof to be exchanged for products made mostly in Mexico or the Far East. Some of these were edged weapons, holiday finery, Puebla ware or majolica, religious books, prints, medals, rosaries and images, porcelain dishes, silks and trinkets from the Spanish Orient. When cheap British goods were added to Chihuahua Fair stocks of merchandise, cottage pottery ware, creamware, spatter ware, feather-edged and lusterware, stoneware, and printed or transfer ware, common in England and the eastern Atlantic states, found their way into New Mexico. Broken bits of these are found on ruined Spanish sites in New Mexico today. With them came Sheffield knives, razors and small hand tools, and bales of woolen and cotton fabrics. A finespun woolen baize made in several British mills went by the trade name of Manchester cloth and was ordered for Mexican use to make up into clothing. It soon found a secondary purpose; weavers liked the colors and quality of the yarn and raveled new bolts of cloth, respinning it to weave into blankets.

Traveling boxes for these luxuries were of two kinds: the painted wooden box made in northern Mexico and the leather-covered Chinese chest. The former, which might have a flat or hutch top, was painted on the sides with panels showing architectural vistas, such as a complete town plaza populated with tiny groups of people, horses, and dogs, framed by borders of flowers and leaves. These decorations were done by skilled craftsmen in slick-surfaced, enameled colors.

Chinese leather chests came nested in various sizes in the latter part of the 18th century. Stretched over a wooden box, the leather was painted red, blue, green, black, or yellow, with bands of painted contrasting decoration, usually floral. It was fastened on by brass bindings and brass-

Jerga, homespun carpet in
diamond weave called *ojo de
perdiz* or partridge eye pattern.
(Page 18)

headed tacks. Even after Mexican independence, such chests continued to arrive in Chihuahua, and in California via Hawaii. If the leather box was no novelty to New Mexicans, the painted box was, and other chests were soon being made of local pine. Some of these were decorated by what is thought to have been a Mexican itinerant artist who carried his oil paints with him. Not so proficient as the Chihuahua painters, he still had a facile brush stroke as surviving panels by him will attest. Homemade painted boxes do not feature whole vistas, but do show men on horseback, in a coach, in boats (certainly not a common New Mexican scene), dancing with ladies, fighting a bull, and lancing a buffalo. Because of the lack of actual surviving garments, these paintings give a valuable record of costume in New Mexico in the first half of the 19th century.

If the top hat and long trousers were invented by Regency dandies, they were slow in reaching our frontier. Long trousers came into Mexico via European military uniforms by 1820-25 and certainly did not instantly affect Santa Fe. Most, if not all, of the men shown on painted chests wear long trousers and so the painting may be assumed to have been done about 1830. These boxes painted with nonreligious scenes seem to have supplied the first examples of human images not devoted to heavenly matters that New Mexican folk painters had seen. They may have been the inspiration for a painted panel on a door which in typical *santero* style of brushwork shows the *cibolero*, or buffalo hunter, with his horse, a contemporary record of the buffalo hunter's dress, horse, and type of saddle, bridle, and spear, which is at present unique and was a milestone in its day.

Mexican rule, although politically separated from Spain, made so little change in New Mexican life that it is hardly worth while to classify frontier folk art created between 1821 and 1846 by any name other than "colonial." Men took to calling each other citizen instead of *don* for a while, but real representation in Mexico or progress at home did not materialize. Lumped together with Chihuahua and Coahuila as the Internal Province of the North, New Mexico for a while lost her identity. Internal struggles in Mexico between dictators and republican elements left the frontier to its own devices and to the rapacity of a local tyrant, Governor Armijo, until the United States took over the West to the Pacific coast.

Ornamentation of crosses, boxes
and candle sconces was often
of tiny bits of wheat straw.
(Page 12)

A new folk craft sprang up in New Mexico when tin containers brought first by traders and later by the United States Army were emptied and thrown away. They were salvaged by New Mexicans, cut up and reworked into fantastically elaborate frames and shrines for the holy images. The limitations of salvage materials often required much more labor in piecing and soldering than would the same pieces had they been made from whole sheet tin. Glass panes and printed wallpaper were also new luxuries, and scraps of both combined with tin made eye-catching constructions. Early tin frames often bear stamped brand names from the factory which sold its products in the cans, but have the shape and style of Federal or Duncan Phyfe wooden mirror frames with side pilasters, corner bosses, and a lunette at the top. Instead of the Federal eagle the tin pediment was stamped with a shell, or three shells, or three rosettes in allusion to baptism and the Holy Trinity. Stamping was done with nail points, a cold chisel, and a few small design elements on dies already in use for leather tooling and silverwork.

If a tinsmith had no glass, he glazed a frame with thin sheets of native mica; fragile stuff, this has hardly survived until today. If no wallpaper borders were available, he painted designs of roses and wavy colored lines on paper to lay under glass panels set into tin. The effect of so much color and glitter was much admired. Tin was used lavishly in the same way that silver had been in Mexico (but silver had never been within reach in New Mexico in sufficient amounts). Today the makeshift painted panels in these tins are preferred by collectors to those with wallpaper, but a century ago it was the other way about.

The small, delicately patterned stamping on earlier tins, as much as their overall shape, indicates their relative age. When railroads, after 1880, brought commercial goods in quantity, wagon and house paints were carried in general stores. This was the Waterloo of native folk arts. New tins were cut in flamboyant shapes and fine stamping was abandoned in favor of red, green, and other oil-paint blobs smeared over the surface. Only occasionally did a craftsman turn out a well-made, tasteful piece of tin after the house-paint era. Tin, glass, and paper trinket boxes were items

Country made chair and table
showing early 19th century
design influence.
(Page 44)

which shed religious association; colored trade cards and catalog covers were laid into these, advertising cough syrup, boots and shoes, or Mumm's champagne.

Eastern furniture brought to New Mexico inaugurated an era of keeping up with the Joneses. If every Spanish family could not order square pianos, Belter chairs, and marble-top tables from St. Louis, the local wood-carver could make acceptable versions of these from pine. In fact, country-made pieces, copying Duncan Phyfe sleigh beds, side chairs, and wash-stands, were the earliest New Mexico departures from their long-established Spanish models. Through the 19th century, versions of spool tables and beds, the sarcophagus style of Victorian double bed, the ginger-bread style and even Eastlake were made in pine and painted, mostly black or barn red. With the chairs came tables of standard height made along time-honored lines, mortised and pegged and decorated with spindle rails or scrolled aprons. It is only the size that indicates a post-annexation piece. The ubiquitous ironing table of eastern households, a bench whose back swung on a pair of dowels, so that it made either a large-topped table or a bench in which sadirons, clothesline and pins were stored, was adopted by New Mexicans. It was usually made in smaller sizes than those of American origin and gaily chip-carved and painted. Like other regional articles, it has somehow acquired in recent years the label of "priest chair" although it was never anything of the sort.

The *trastero*, for so long the family pride, came to a sad end. New models of these aped the Yankee "meat safe," plainly assembled cupboards of deal with panels of punched tin meant to let air in and keep flies out. The tin, already dear to New Mexicans, was decorated as usual and added more shiny surface to the kitchen.

Textiles in the 19th century went through a cycle of beauty and decline. Prior to the introduction of Germantown yarns and commercial dyes, weaving had been of handspun and vegetable-dyed materials. Patterns had a subtle variety within a framework of bands, stripes, and lozenges, and the gamut of indigo, red, rose, yellows, and tans with natural-colored yarns. With a greater range of commercial dyes, an urge for more intricate patterns arose. Their complicated designs set off the new color range, not always with happy results. While the multicolored, busy designs were at their height, a crippled woman named Patricia Montoya of El Valle, a tiny village in the mountains, made blankets with gay eight-pointed stars combined with lozenges, zigzags, ticked borders, and whatever else she could include. The starry blankets are known as *Valleros*.

Rambouillet sheep were brought in by new sheepmen for their hardiness and larger wool clip, but the wool was coarse and brittle. Spun into yarn, it did not equal the light, silky Merino product, so textiles grew poor in quality. Some *gringo* ladies introduced the arts of hooking and weaving rags. Of these there had always been enough, but rags hooked into rosettes in the midst of a wool-embroidered *colcha* date the piece as probably post-1860. Wool warps and rag wefts woven into *jerga* were tried out but did not prove durable. Old looms were still used to make rag rugs in many places, but weaving died out as a craft except in Taos and Rio Arriba counties and the San Luis Valley where it has continued into our time. In about 1900, cotton warps were adopted and this was the end of good Spanish weaving.

Pine love seat. (Page 44)

POSTSCRIPT

Any culture pattern will disintegrate when another is superimposed upon it by newcomers with different language, religious practices, values, and standards of behavior. Even though the previous pattern, in the eyes of impartial observers, offered more rewarding ways of living and moral and aesthetic values, the new culture, especially when it dominates the economy, supplants the old.

It has been pointed out in the foregoing summary of colonial artifacts that new material goods could be absorbed by a population without much disturbance of their scale of values. The Spanish New Mexicans commissioned and received the greatest number of country-made *santos* for church and home during the period when new types of goods were coming into their lives for the first time from Chihuahua and the Missouri warehouses.

However, after new influences reached them from Catholic pastors of their own faith if not of the same linguistic background, the shield of unified Hispanic solidarity began to crack. New forms of political machinery, new kinds of jobs, and the preaching of progress made a period of self-conscious inferiority inevitable. If primitive methods, poverty, and illiteracy were to be abolished, arts and crafts were swept out with them as a part of the old inferior life. In the destruction of these, dignity and contentment die too, and the conqueror and missionary seldom provide equivalent substitutes for the intangibles they have wrecked.

History repeatedly records that after a phase of turning old ways upside down, the newcomers, having settled down to their program as the only possible one, begin unconsciously to absorb and enjoy some part of the aesthetics of the people whom they are trying to make over. This has happened in New Mexico after a century or so of dual interests. If the first to deny symbolist saints and hand-hewn chests were the Spanish, the first to begin to collect and reproduce these were the "Anglos." Artists, writers, and other people began to collect the indigo blankets, the stately *trastero*, straw-covered boxes, tin sconces and, most of all, the *santos*. Today examples of these and many more related colonial crafts of New Mexico are owned by twenty-two museums in the United States, excluding

Tin and glass shrine or *nicho* with miniature figures depicting *"el gran poder de Dios"* or the great power of God. (Collection of Charles D. Carroll).

(Page 42)

New Mexico, and in Berlin, Tokyo, and other parts of the globe. Private collections exist from Florida to California. Second only to the American Indian, the *santero* and his associated craftsmen are recognized as creators of the most original popular art ever developed in what is now the United States.

REFERENCES CITED IN THE TEXT

1. MAGOFFIN, Susan Shelby.
   Down the Santa Fe Trail and into Mexico: the Diary of Susan Shelby Magoffin, 1846-47. New Haven, 1926.

2. DOMINGUEZ, Fray Francisco Atanasio.
   The Missions of New Mexico, 1776, A Description by Fray Francisco Atanasio Dominguez, with other contemporary documents. Translated and annotated by Eleanor B. Adams and Fray Angelico Chavez, Albuquerque, 1956.

3. *Una Casa del Siglo XVIII en Mexico, La del Conde de San Bartolomé de Xala.* Edited by Manuel Romero de Torreros, Mexico, 1957.

4. *Spanish Archives of New Mexico.* Edited by Ralph E. Twitchell, Cedar Rapids, 1914.

5. *Archives of the Archdiocese of Santa Fe.* Unpublished documents quoted by gracious permission of his Excellency the Archbishop of Santa Fe.

6. EMERY, Irene.
   Wool Embroideries of New Mexico; Some Notes on the Stitch Employed. El Palacio, V. 56, No. 11, Nov. 1949.

7. GETTENS, John Rutherford.
   The Materials and Methods of Some Religious Paintings of Early Nineteenth Century New Mexico. El Palacio, V. 58, No. 1, Jan. 1951.

8. WILDER, Mitchell A. and BREITENBACH, Edgar.
   Santos, the Religious Folk Art of New Mexico. Colorado Springs, 1943.

PHOTOGRAPHY
    Color plates by Eliot Porter
    Black and white plates by Laura Gilpin

SOURCES
    Unless otherwise noted the objects
    reproduced are from the Spanish Colonial
    collections of the Museum of New Mexico.

VERGARA PRINTING COMPANY
Santa Fe, New Mexico